D1328825

Charlie Brown

and Snoopy

Selected Cartoons from AS YOU LIKE IT,
CHARLIE BROWN, Vol. 1

Charles M. Schulz

CORONET BOOKS
Hodder Fawcett Ltd., London

Printed and bound in Great Britain for
Coronet Books,
Hodder Fawcett Ltd,
St. Paul's House, Warwick Lane,
London, EC4P 4AH
by Hazell Watson & Viney Ltd,
Aylesbury, Bucks

ISBN 0 340 12520 9

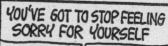

HERE, SNOOPY.. CHASE THE STICK!

I'LL BET IF YOU TRIED IT ONCE YOU'D THINK IT WAS FUN

THAT'S WHY I DON'T WANT TO START... I'M AFRAID I MIGHT ENJOY IT!

YOU WON'T DO IT, HUH?

NOPE!

I WANT PEOPLE TO HAVE MORE TO SAY ABOUT ME AFTER I'M GONE THAN, "HE WAS A NICE GUY... HE CHASED STICKS!"

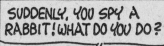

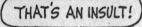

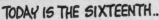

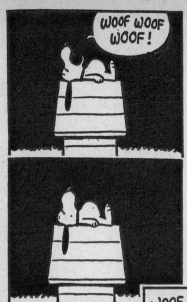

STUPID DOG!

THAT'S HIS "HA HA..YOU HAVE TO GO TO SCHOOL, AND I DON'T" DANCE!

SNOOPY'S IN THE HOSPITAL?

UH HUH...DIDN'T YOU KNOW? HE'S BEEN THERE FOR ABOUT FOUR DAYS...

IS HE ALLOWED TO HAVE VISITORS?

OH, YES...HE'S HAD A FEW CLOSE FRIENDS DROP BY ALREADY...

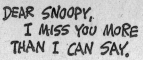

DEAR SNOOPY,
I MISS YOU MORE THAN I CAN SAY.

I HOPE THEY ARE TREATING YOU WELL IN THE HOSPITAL.

WHILE YOU ARE THERE, WHY DON'T YOU HAVE THEM GIVE YOU A FLEA BATH?

I SAY THIS, OF COURSE, AT THE RISK OF BEING OFFENSIVE. HOPING TO SEE YOU SOON. YOUR PAL,
CHARLIE BROWN

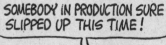

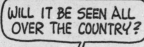

WHAT ARE YOU DOING?

THIS IS A PROJECTOR FOR OBSERVING THE ECLIPSE TOMORROW..

THERE IS NO SAFE METHOD FOR LOOKING DIRECTLY AT AN ECLIPSE, AND IT IS ESPECIALLY DANGEROUS WHEN IT IS A TOTAL ECLIPSE...

THEREFORE, I'VE TAKEN TWO PIECES OF WHITE CARDBOARD, AND PUT A PINHOLE IN ONE.. THIS WILL SERVE TO PROJECT THE IMAGE ONTO THE OTHER BOARD.. SEE?

I'LL BET BEETHOVEN NEVER WOULD HAVE THOUGHT OF THAT!

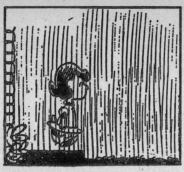

7

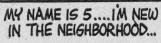

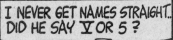

I THINK MOST OF US TAKE NEWSPAPERS TOO MUCH FOR GRANTED..

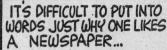

WE DON'T REALLY APPRECIATE THE MIRACLE THAT IS THE MODERN DAILY NEWSPAPER...

IT'S DIFFICULT TO PUT INTO WORDS JUST WHY ONE LIKES A NEWSPAPER...

I LIKE A NEWSPAPER BECAUSE YOU DON'T HAVE TO DIAL IT!

WHAT ARE YOU READING?

THIS IS AN ADAPTATION OF SHERLOCK HOLMES...

AN "ADAPTATION"?

YES, IT'S BEEN "ADAPTED" FOR CHILDREN...

IT'S NOT UNLIKE DRINKING DILUTED ROOT BEER!

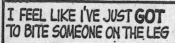

ONCE THERE WAS A TIME WHEN I THOUGHT I COULD GIVE UP THUMB-SUCKING...

NOW I DOUBT IF I EVER COULD...

I'M HOOKED!

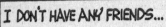

DON'T TELL ME YOU'RE SITTING HERE WAITING FOR THE "GREAT PUMPKIN" AGAIN?

HOW CAN YOU BELIEVE IN SOMETHING THAT JUST ISN'T TRUE? HE'S NEVER GOING TO SHOW UP! HE DOESN'T EXIST!

WHEN YOU STOP BELIEVING IN THAT FELLOW WITH THE RED SUIT AND WHITE BEARD WHO GOES, "HO HO HO", I'LL STOP BELIEVING IN THE "GREAT PUMPKIN"!

WE ARE OBVIOUSLY SEPARATED BY DENOMINATIONAL DIFFERENCES!

DEAR SANTA,
   HERE IS A LIST OF
WHAT I WANT.

HOW DO YOU SUPPOSE SANTA CLAUS CAN AFFORD TO GIVE AWAY ALL THOSE TOYS?

PROMOTION! DON'T KID YOURSELF....EVERYTHING THESE DAYS IS PROMOTION!

I'LL BET IF THE TRUTH WERE BROUGHT OUT, YOU'D FIND THAT HE'S BEING FINANCED BY SOME BIG EASTERN CHAIN!